ABC Animal RIDDLES

by Susan Joyce

illustrations by Doug DuBosque

Peel Productions, Inc.

Text copyright©1999 Susan Joyce
Illustrations & design
copyright©1999 Doug DuBosque
All rights reserved.

Published by Peel Productions, Inc.
PO Box 546, Columbus NC 28722

http://peelbooks.com

Printed & bound in Hong Kong

L_____y of Congress
Cataloging-in-publication data

Joyce, Susan, 1945–
ABC animal riddles / by Susan Joyce ; illustrations by
   Doug DuBosque
   p.   cm.
Summary: Rhyming alphabet-based riddles challenge
the reader to identify animals from clues, including
the first and last letter of the word.
ISBN 0-939217-51-1 (alk. paper)
1. Riddles, Juvenile.   [1. Riddles. 2. Animals. 3.
Alphabet.]   I. DuBosque, D. C., ill. II. Title.

PN6371.5.J677 1999
818'.5402–dc21

98-42518

a _ t

I start with an A and end with a T.
My family lives
in a big colony.
We are ruled by a queen,
who is not often seen.
She lays eggs continuously.
Can you name me?

b _ _ _ _ r

My name has six letters.
It starts with a B.
With my very large teeth,
I can cut down a tree.
I build dams with a mix
of mud, stone and sticks.
I'm a rodent. I'm furry.
What can I be?

C _ _ _ L

I start with a C and end with an L.
I live in the desert,
a hard place to dwell.
When I'm feeding well,
my large hump will swell.
If I have two humps,
they swell as well.
I carry people,
or goods that they sell.
What am I? Can you tell?

d — k

I start with a D and end with a K.
My flat bill is perfect
for dabbling all day.
To keep my feathers clean,
I preen and preen and preen.
I waddle when I walk.
I quack when I talk.
What's my name? Can you say?

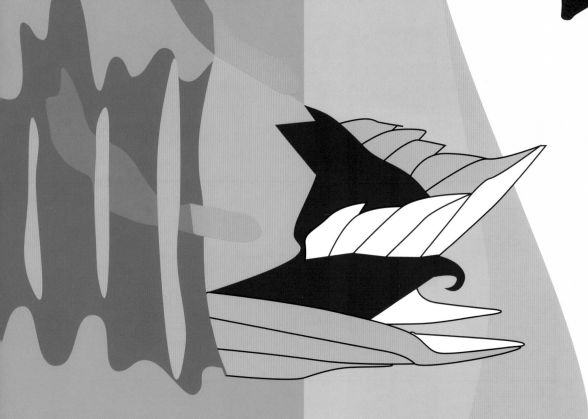

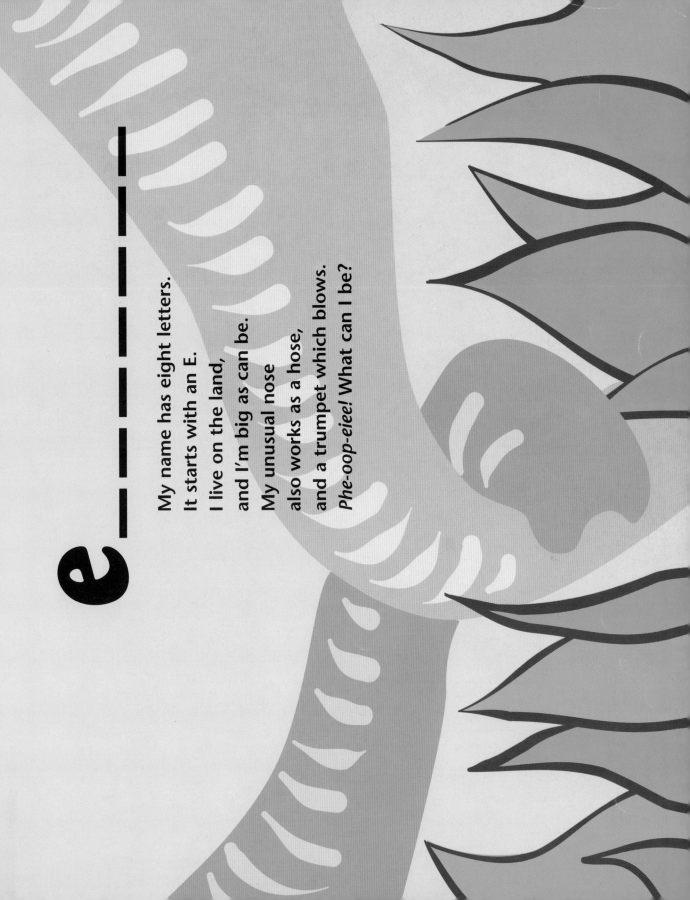

e — — — —

My name has eight letters.
It starts with an E.
I live on the land,
and I'm big as can be.
My unusual nose
also works as a hose,
and a trumpet which blows.
Phe-oop-eiee! What can I be?

I start with an F and end with a Y.
When it's light out, I hide.
When it grows dark, I fly.
I dance and flash my light—
five flashes, green and bright.
I let female beetles know
I'm watching for their glow.
What am I? Do you know?

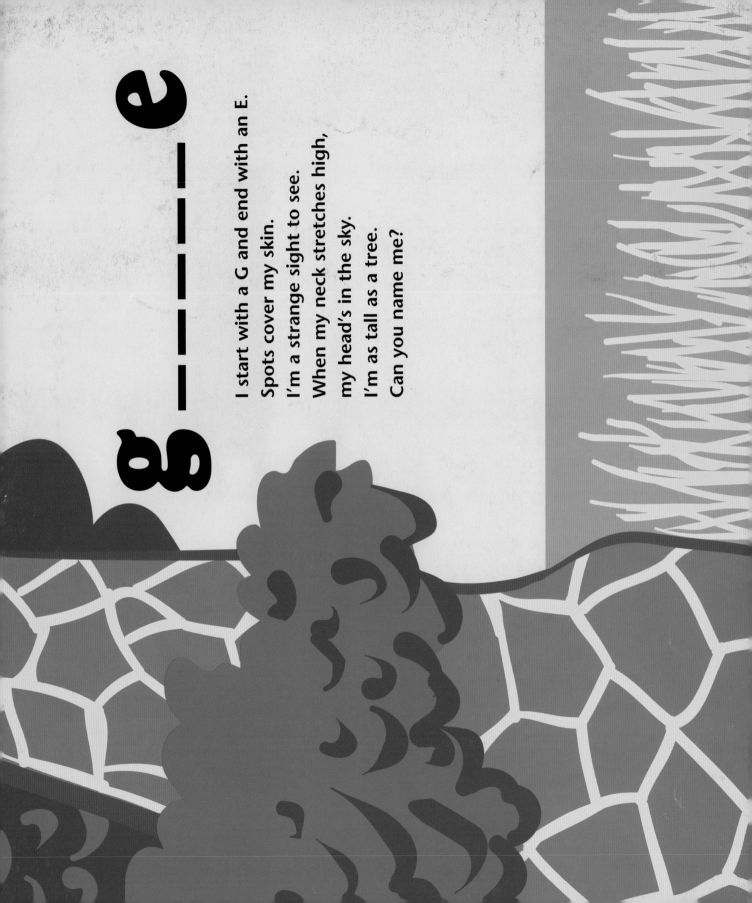

g - - - - e

I start with a G and end with an E.
Spots cover my skin.
I'm a strange sight to see.
When my neck stretches high,
my head's in the sky.
I'm as tall as a tree.
Can you name me?

h- - - - - - - s

I start with an H and end with an S.
My barrel-shaped body
is almost hairless.
I'm related to the pig,
but I'm really, REALLY BIG!
I swim and laze all day.
At night I graze away.
What am I? Can you say?